Christmas,

A Happy Time

MISS MANT

[ZHINGOORA BOOKS]

This edition is published by
Zhingoora Books.

The Cover is Designed by Pallav Sethiya.

CHRISTMAS,

A HAPPY TIME.

Harriet and Elizabeth Mortimer were two very pretty, and generally speaking, very good little girls. Their kind papa and mamma had taken a great deal of pains that they should be good, and it was very seldom that they vexed them by being otherwise. A very happy time was now expected in the family at Beech Grove, by the arrival of John and Frederick Mortimer from school: it was within a few days of Christmas; and as the sisters and brothers had never, till the last few months, been separated, their meeting together again was looked forward to with general and lively pleasure.

'Do you see anything of the stage, Elizabeth?' said Harriet to her sister, who had been running down to the end of the plantation to peep over the gate, and listen if she could hear the approach of wheels.

'No: there is nothing in sight,' replied Elizabeth, whose teeth chattered from the cold, while her hands were so benumbed, she could scarcely close the gate, which she had ventured to open about half an inch.

'They will never come,' said Harriet; 'but you should not open the gate, you know papa and mamma both told us we should not do that. And how cold you are! you are all over in a shiver. Come let us have a run round, and that will warm you. Remember mamma begged of us not to stand still in this sharp cutting wind.'

'Yes, so she did,' replied Elizabeth; 'and indeed it is very, very cold, down at that corner. And they will not come any the sooner for our standing there.'

And according to Harriet's proposal, the two little girls began to run round the grounds, which put them in a complete glow; and Elizabeth's fingers very soon ceased to ache with cold.

As they passed the green house, they saw the gardener matting up some myrtles on the outside; and Elizabeth stopped, to enquire at what time the coach was likely to pass.

'I look for it every minute, Miss,' replied the man; 'and that's the reason I keep about here, that I may be handy to help the young gentlemen out, and bring in the boxes and that. I look for them to be much grown, Miss, for 'tis a fine bit now since we have seen them. I don't know what Master John will say about his myrtle that he used to be so proud of, for I am afraid its dead. But hark ye, Miss—sure that's wheels.—Yes, and there comes a coach too.'

And away posted the gardener, and both the little girls after him.

It was a coach; and it was a very noisy one, or at least the passengers were very noisy. Such a blowing of horns, and hallooing and huzzaing. But the coach went by without stopping at the gate; and although the gardener ran after it, and endeavoured to speak with the coachman, his voice was drowned in the multitude of little voices within and without the coach; and he was obliged to return, disappointed himself, to the disappointed young ladies, who stood anxiously looking out, within the gate.

Before there was time to express any regret, another coach appeared in sight, and this might be the coach so much longed for. This also approached with shouting and blowing of horns; again the gardener put himself forward and this time the coach seemed to draw down towards the gate. Harriet even fancied she saw her dear brother John looking out of one of the windows. But again she was disappointed. The coachman, though he drew to the side of the road, scarcely allowed his horses to stop; and flinging the servant a letter, which he took from his waistcoat pocket, again he flourished his whip, and again the coach passed on.

'A letter for your papa, Miss,' said the gardener, picking it up and offering it to the young ladies: 'Shall I take it to James to carry in?'

'No; I will—I will,' exclaimed both the little girls at once. Elizabeth, though the youngest, generally contrived to be forwardest; and seizing upon the letter, as the gardener held it between his finger and thumb, she scampered away, followed by Harriet, and they both arrived almost breathless in the drawing-room.

'The coaches are both past, papa,' said Harriet, 'without John and Frederick'; and as soon as the information had been given, she burst into tears.

'But here is a letter, which will tell about it, I dare say, papa,' added Elizabeth. 'To John Mortimer, Esq. Beech Grove,' she continued, reading the direction, as she presented the letter. 'It is John's writing, papa.'

Mrs. Mortimer looked uneasy; and Mr. Mortimer broke the seal of the letter with some little alarm.

'It is all well,' said the kind father, almost directly; 'nothing to apprehend, my love,' added he, as he handed the letter across to his wife.

The letter was as follows:—

My Dear Papa,

No room for us in either of the coaches—inside or out. Mr. Brown is going to send us in a post chaise, with two other boys.

Your affectionate and dutiful Son,

JOHN MORTIMER.

'Our pleasure is only delayed for a few hours,' said Mr. Mortimer, as he put an arm round the neck of each of his little girls. 'They will be here in the course of a short time, no doubt, and have you got every thing ready to receive them?'

'Oh yes, papa, quite ready,' replied Elizabeth, who was slipping her neck from under her father's arm, with the intention of again returning to the bottom of the shrubbery. Harriet directly followed her towards the door.

'And where now my little girls,' said Mrs. Mortimer; 'not to the shrubbery again this evening?'

'We were going, mamma,' replied Elizabeth: 'had you rather we should not?'

'I had,' answered Mrs. Mortimer; you have been out nearly two hours, and the air is now very sharp and cold; the sun is set, and in a short time it will be quite dusk. You can watch the road from the play-room window; and I think it very likely your brothers will not be here before quite night.'

Both the little girls would have preferred another run in the shrubbery, and another peep over the gate at the end of it: but they were accustomed to know, that their mother's judgment was better than their own; and without a murmur, therefore they repaired to the school-room.

'Oh! there they are,—there they are,' said Elizabeth, before she had scarcely reached the window: 'It must be my brothers,—I am sure it was a post-chaise.'

'Where—where?' said Harriet, jumping up upon the window seat, and straining her eyes to catch a sight of the desired object.

'I cannot see it now,' replied Elizabeth, 'it is gone behind the elm trees by the side of the road: we shall see it again, presently. Do go, dear Harriet, and ask mamma if we may go down and meet them.'

'But I do not know they are coming,' said Harriet: 'do dear Elizabeth tell me where you saw them. I do not think you could have seen them: and if you did, they must be a great way off.'

'Oh there—there, Harriet, cannot you see them now?' said Elizabeth, putting her arm round her sister's neck; 'There,—just by the mill, this side of the elms. Now they are gone again.'

'Yes, I see them,' replied Harriet; 'and now they are come out again from behind old Jackson's cottage. Oh, now I see them very plain.—I can almost make them both out.'

'Oh, I can make them *quite* out,' said Elizabeth; 'and they have got a horn, too, and are blowing away: and John is shaking his handkerchief. Oh, I wish we might go down and meet them.'

And both the children began jumping about in an ecstasy of joy. At this moment Mr. and Mrs. Mortimer entered the play-room. 'They are coming, papa,—they are coming, mamma,' said Harriet and Elizabeth both together. Mrs. Mortimer had thrown a large cloak and hood over her, and Mr. Mortimer had his hat in his hand.

'We were coming to fetch you to meet them,' said Mr. Mortimer.— 'Come, make haste, or they will be here before we can be out of the house; for the young gentlemen travel rapidly with their four horses.'

Harriet and Elizabeth hastened after their father and mother, who were preparing to lead the way to the shrubbery, but before they were out of the hall door, the post chaise and four was rattling down the avenue and in a few minutes the two lads were pressed to the hearts of their beloved parents and their affectionate sisters.

As the two other youths who accompanied the Mortimers were eager to pursue their journey, the chaise was soon on its return down the avenue: and John and Frederick, who with all their happiness, could not help finding out that they were very cold and hungry, were glad to be summoned to the dining-room, and to feel the warm carpet, and see the blazing fire, and the smoking meat upon the table. Between eating and talking there was a great deal to do; the former, however, it was most necessary to attend to for a short time; and when their hunger was satisfied, and they drew with their father and mother, and Elizabeth and Harriet, round the cheerful and enlivening fire, and a more happy party perhaps could hardly be imagined. Before the boys went to school, each of the children had low stools of their own, which it had always been their delight to sit upon, when summoned to the dining-room after dinner; for at that time they had been accustomed to have their own dinner in the nursery. Now, however, they were to be indulged by dining with their parents, when the family dinner hour was moderately early, and there was no large party at table; and on the present occasion the same little stools which had been such favourites formerly were now brought again into use. The girls had almost feared proposing them, as they knew not what changes the *boy's school* might have occasioned in their brother's habits; but no sooner was the cloth removed and the grace said, than the active little Frederick flew to the sideboard, and took possession of his old and favourite seat. John followed his example; those of the two little girls were already standing by the two corners of the chimney-piece, and Frederick between mamma and Elizabeth, and John between papa and Harriet, very soon settled themselves and made the family circle complete. Into the middle of this circle a favourite little terrier now leaped, and began his gambols, while the old pet Tibby the cat, which the children had all been accustomed to carry about from infants, came rubbing her sides against the young strangers, and began purring to be taken notice of.

As the day had closed long before the dinner had disappeared, the boys could only hear all there was to be heard to-night, about any alterations or improvements which had taken place since their absence;—what success their sisters had met with, in keeping up their stock of rabbits and poultry;—whether the ice-house had been yet filled;—how went on old Neddy the donkey, if he was yet too old to be ridden;—whether the myrtles were alive, and their own gardens had been full of flowers; and a variety of other inquiries, extremely interesting to them, and which would have doubtless been made by many of my young readers on similar occasions as those on which we are writing. Harriet and Elizabeth were equally glad to reply to all their brothers' questions, and they had a great many to ask in return. Whether they liked school as well as home,—whether they always had meat and pudding, & as much as they liked of both;—what plays they played at, and if they had good-natured companions. There was an abundance to say upon all these subjects; and then Mr. and Mrs. Mortimer had their inquiries to make about books and classes, and sums, and school hours, and play hours and going to bed, and getting up, so that the tongues all ran very nimbly; and doubtless there remained plenty more to say, when at length little Frederick's words began to lengthen themselves as he uttered them, and his eyes were with difficulty strained open.

Mr. Mortimer gave him a pat, and asked him how early he had been up in the morning? He had scarcely been in bed the whole night; he had since performed a journey of near seventy miles, and as he was not yet seven years of age, it was not to be wondered at that sleep should thus be striving to get the better even of his feelings of joy and happiness, John, who was only two years older than his brother did not shew much less symptoms of fatigue; and Mrs. Mortimer proposed having the tea immediately, that the boys might get to bed. This plan was instantly agreed to, their heads were soon snug on their pillows; and in the morning they both awoke in high health and joyous spirits.

It was now that Mr. and Mrs. Mortimer could see how much their dear boys were grown, and how well they were looking. John triumphantly stood beside his sister Harriet, who was a year older than himself, and told her he should be very soon taller than she was; and Frederick had actually out-stripped the little Elizabeth, who told one more year than he did. The girls however were reconciled to this acquired superiority of stature, by discovering that papa was a great deal taller than mamma, though they were both exactly the same age; and Frederick concluded the whole dissertation, by adding that to be sure, men ought be taller than women.

'It does not much signify what are your heights, my dear children,' said Mr. Mortimer, affectionately gazing upon the whole group, 'if you are but good and amiable. I should be very glad to see my young Fred a brave grenadier,' added the fond father placing his hand upon the head of his young son: 'but I shall be much better pleased to see him a good man. But now who is for a walk?—the morning is bright and fair, and those who do not mind the cold, away for your great coats and hats, and I will take a walk with you to the ice-house, and see if the men are beginning to fill it.'

It was not necessary to repeat this invitation, and towards the ice-house the party immediately proceeded. As they passed through the park they went by a sheet of water, on which during the summer, had been a boat, but which now was caked over with ice, and had every appearance of being hard enough to bear the weight of a man with his skates on. John and Frederick were both running to the edge: and had not their father been with them would have immediately ventured on an amusement, hardy and bracing when followed with prudence, but which requires the caution of experience, not to be carelessly indulged in.

'Wait till to-morrow, boys,' said Mr. Mortimer, 'the ice is not strong enough to bear you to-day. In another four and twenty hours, I think it will be safe, should the frost continue, and I have directed James to prepare my skates.'

The boys both desisted, for they had been very early taught to submit to the opinion of their father: but Frederick could not help saying, 'I think it *would* bear, papa:' and feeling more disappointment than his looks perhaps expressed.

'We can very well wait another day, Frederick,' said John, as he saw his brother's disappointment on walking on.

'Perhaps the frost may be broken then,' replied Frederick; but he soon found other amusement, and bounded over the stile into the lane, before the rest of the party had scarcely lost sight of the sheet of water in the park.

'Oh, here are the men with a load,' said Frederick, as his father came in sight, 'fine thick ice, papa—oh, so thick, I am sure it must be hard enough to slide where that thick ice comes from.'

'That ice is taken from a mere hole,' replied Mr. Mortimer: 'from that dirty little patch of water by the side of yonder hedge—do you see? It is very shallow, and is therefore soon encrusted: but even before it was cut by the pickaxe, it would not have been smooth enough to have slidden upon, and now you see it is all in pieces, and you might as well try to slide on a heap of stones.'

By this time all the party had crossed the stile, and were proceeding along the lane.

'I wonder you do not have the ice-house filled from the water in the park papa' said Harriet. 'This is such dirty, nasty-looking stuff.'

'You have before seen in what manner the ice-house is filled,' replied Mr. Mortimer; 'that the ice is all broken, almost pounded to pieces, and then stored below ground; and I have also told you that it is never eaten, and it signifies little whether it is entirely pure or not. The house will be rendered as cold by this ice, as by that from the park, and that is all which is necessary. And it would be a pity to spoil the appearance of the other, unless it were necessary; particularly as John and Frederick and myself hope to have same good slides upon it during the holidays.'

Having stopped to ask a few questions of the men employed in conveying the ice from the pond, Mr. Mortimer now proceeded with his children to a farm-house not very far distant, where they all met a very hearty welcome, and where the boys' attention was arrested by two little grey ponies, which were in the meadow adjoining the farm yard.

'Well—what do you think of them,' said Mr. Mortimer. They were pronounced beautiful by both the boys, and their father then told them they had been purchased for their use, and that of their sisters; but that they would not be fit to be ridden till the summer. He designed to have them properly broken in by the next holidays, and the boys were delighted with the prospect of riding them on their next return from school.

'If the young gentlemen would like a ride this Christmas, Sir,' said the kind farmer, 'my Thomas's poney is a nice quiet little fellow, and Tom would be proud to lend him.' John and Frederick looked at each other, and at their father, but at length John suggested, that as only one could ride at a time they had better put off their rides till the summer; and Harriet and Elizabeth were both pleased that such was the decision.

The next visit was to the parsonage, where many a round happy countenance greeted the return of the young Mortimers: and while Mr. Mortimer was engaged in conversation with the excellent pastor of the village, Mr. Wexford, the young people were introduced into the play-room of the little Wexfords. Mr. Wexford made a petition that the young people should spend the day together: but as it was the first of the Mortimers being at home, their father declined it for them, at the same time promising that they should have the indulgence in a short time: and also expressing a hope that the Wexfords would return the visit at Beech Grove.

At that time of the year there was little to be seen out of doors, but one curiosity the Wexfords described, to which they were very anxious to introduce their young friends: and this was a little group of robin red-breasts which had been hatched in their summer-house, and which now took shelter there every night, and were regularly fed by the family.

'The gardener says they do not do us much good,' said Maria Wexford, as they approached the summer house; 'but I do not like that they should be destroyed.'

'Oh no, I could not have them destroyed,' replied Harriet Mortimer, 'even if they spoiled my flowers, they are such pretty creatures. But where are John and Frederick?'

John and Frederick had scampered off with the young Wexfords, and presently returned with a pan of bread crumbs, which they had begged from the cook, and which they now hoped to see the red-breasts eat.

But the little creatures were alarmed at seeing so many visitors; or the sun enticed them to extend their flight beyond the green house; for on the entrance of the boys, they all took wing and flew away.

'I am sorry we frightened them,' said Harriet.

'Do you not think they will ever come back again?' asked Elizabeth.

'Oh yes, they will be back in the evening or before,' replied Maria Wexford; 'they often fly out in the day-time when it is fine. But perhaps you would like to run round the garden; you will be cold standing still.'

The party was preparing for a race when Mr. Mortimer appeared to summon that part of it which belonged to him; and, having arranged a day with Mr. Wexford, for the families to meet at Beech Grove, Mr. Mortimer and his children returned towards the park.

As they approached the sheet of water, which Frederick again surveyed with a longing eye, they perceived that Mr. Wexford's large Newfoundland dog had followed them from the parsonage, and the boys directly began throwing stones and sticks before them for the animal to run after and bring back to them.

This dog was particularly fond of the water, and John having thrown a stick to the edge of it, it had slipped over the side and the fine animal immediately sprang after it. The boys for an instant were both inclined to smile at the animal's finding footing, when he had expected to sink in the water, but they both turned pale, and looked at their father, when they almost immediately saw him disappear under the ice. It had been so partially frozen that the weight of the dog in plunging, had broken it, and he had sunk to rise no more. Mr Mortimer's heart sickened as he contemplated what might have been the case had his own children ventured on the ice, and he blessed God that their dispositions were such, as to make them obedient to his wishes. Every means were taken for the recovery of the dog, and after some hours he was extricated from the ice; but he was perfectly dead, and apparently had been so some time.

"They are coming papa, they are coming mamma." see

As Mr. Mortimer and his children continued their walk towards the house, they heard a shrill shouting from the direction of the village;—it seemed like the shouting of young voices, and was evidently that of joyfulness. The attention of the children was immediately attracted towards it, and Mr. Mortimer indulged them by moving in its direction. John and Frederick were very soon out of sight, and in a few minutes they returned to relate the cause of the acclamations they had heard. They proceeded from the children of the parish school, who had just been dismissed by their master and mistress, and were to be treated with a week's holiday. Hurra—hurra—cried all the little noisy fellows, as Mr. Mortimer came up; while the squeaking voices of the little girls joined in the cry, at the same time as they jumped, and danced, and frisked about happy and joyous as little birds. The young Mortimers hastened towards the gate, and as they opened it, the young crowd gave them another hurra; and two or three of the biggest of the boys approached, and making their village nods to the squire, at the same time touching their hats, they offered their Christmas pieces for exhibition. Mr. Mortimer gave these little lads sixpence each, and calling to the gardener to get him a few shillings' worth of halfpence from the village shop, he bade the happy group of children stop a few minutes near the gate. This they were most glad to do, and on the return of the gardener, John and Frederick, commissioned by their father, gave each of the little girls two-pence, and Harriet and Elizabeth had the same pleasing commission to execute towards the boys. All was joy and hilarity; and when Mr. Mortimer told them that on Christmas-day they were to come to his house, to have some beef and plum-pudding, all the little happy countenances shone with delight.

'And now run on, and get home,' said Mr. Mortimer: 'for your parents will be waiting for you at their dinners. And take care you do not get into any mischief in the course of the next week: and if you go out to slide mind that the ice is well hardened before you venture on it. And a merry Christmas to you all.'

'Merry Christmas to *you*, Sir,' replied the biggest boy, who was a very well-spoken lad, and looked as happy, though he made less noise than the rest. 'Merry Christmas—Merry Christmas,' was echoed from a number of little voices around him; and with another joyous shout, the motley group proceeded onwards through the village.

Mr. Mortimer now left his children, and proceeded also through the village where he had himself business to transact. The children went into the house to get their luncheon of bread and jam, and after the girls had rested themselves, their mother promised to take a stroll with them and their brothers round the garden and through the green-houses. At this time of year there was little to see; but still what little there was, was worth seeing, and a stroll with mamma was always a treat.

'What piles of shirts and round frocks! mamma,' said John, while they were eating their luncheon. 'And what numbers of frocks! why, you might set up a shop almost.'

'Cannot you guess what these frocks and shirts are all for?' said Harriet.

'I can,' said the quick little Frederick. 'They are for the children we saw in the lane just now; and they are to have them against Christmas.'

'You are right, Frederick,' replied his mother; 'and I have been taking the opportunity of this holiday of your sisters, to look them over and parcel them out.'

Just now the door opened, and a housemaid appeared with a large basket of shoes and stockings, and another with women's gowns and men's frocks.

'How pleased all the poor people will be, mamma!' said Elizabeth, taking up a gown from the basket; 'it is rather coarse cloth though, I think, mamma.'

'It would be very coarse for you to wear, Elizabeth,' replied Mrs. Mortimer, 'because you are born in a state of affluence, and therefore it is becoming that you should be drest according to the fortune of your papa. But to give fine garments to the poor would be no kindness to them, nor a fit manner of shewing our benevolence towards them.'

'I think papa is very good and kind, do not you, mamma?' said Harriet, looking very steadfastly at her mother.

'Your father has a great pleasure in benefiting any one it is in his power to serve, and is as you observe, Harriet, one of the kindest of men. But he does no more than his duty, and this he would himself tell you, in being a vigilant guardian over the necessities of his poor neighbours. Providence has placed a large fortune at his disposal; and one end of its being given, was, that he might clothe the naked and feed the hungry. Christmas would not be a time of much rejoicing to the poor, were not the rich to assist them in making it so: and I hope all my dear children, while they are enjoying themselves with every comfort and indulgence around them, will be rendered happier by reflecting that the inhabitants of every cottage in the village are rejoicing at the same time.'

'We shall not have a party on Christmas-day, shall we, mamma?' asked John.

'None, excepting our own family, John,' replied Mrs. Mortimer. 'I hope both your uncles will be with us, and your grandpapa and grandmamma have promised to come over from Cannon Hill. The Mortimers from Haversly too I expect, and these I think will complete our circle 'round the Christmas fire.

'Oh, I hope grandpapa will come,' said Frederick, 'because he has always such a number of battles and fighting stories to tell, and he is so droll besides.'

'And I am sure I hope uncle Philip will come,' said Elizabeth; 'for he is so fond of play, and jumping me up to the ceiling.'

'I think you are getting almost too big for this play,' said Mrs. Mortimer; 'and so uncle Philip would feel in his arms, I believe, were he to attempt to jump you now.'

'We shall all dine with you then, mamma, shall we not?' said Elizabeth; 'if there is no other company. You know they are relations, and are all fond of us children.'

'You shall all dine in the room, certainly,' said Mrs. Mortimer; 'but if the four young Mortimers come, I think some of you will be obliged to dine at the side table, but that none of you will mind.'

'Oh, we do not mind that at all, mamma,' said Harriet; 'but we had rather not have any of the Mortimers with us, for they are so rude and noisy, and papa always thinks that we make the noise; and I am sure it is always their fault, though we cannot help laughing at them.'

'You see, in the instance of your cousins, Harriet,' said Mrs. Mortimer, 'the disadvantage of never having any restraint put on little girl's educations. I myself have seen that they occasionally are boisterous and overbearing in their manners; but the fault is not their own. And, if you remember, one day when they were with us, without their own father and mother, they were as orderly and well-behaved as possible.—But will you never have finished your luncheon, Frederick?'

'I was so hungry, mamma,' replied the little boy; 'but I have done now: and now shall we go out again?'

'Did you call on nurse this morning?' said Mrs. Mortimer.

'No, mamma, I quite forgot her,' replied Frederick; 'but we will go now shall we, John, while mamma finishes sorting the things?'

'You must never forget her, my dear boy,' replied the tender mother; 'for without her care of you, when your own mother was too weak to attend to you, you would not have been the stout active boy you now are.'

'I hope you have a nice gown and petticoat for nurse, mamma?' said Frederick.

'She has not been forgotten,' replied Mrs. Mortimer; 'and you shall have the pleasure of carrying the bundle prepared for her yourself. There it is:—the cotton gown, and stuff petticoat, the shoes, stockings, and apron, lying together at the corner of the table.'

Frederick, with a little of his mother's assistance, soon made these separate articles into a bundle; and the two boys set off for Nurse Winscomb's cottage.

The stroll round the garden did not take place on that day; for the boys met their father returning from the cottage of the nurse, and he took them with him to call on a gentleman residing about two miles distant, and whose family were to be invited, with a few others, to meet together in the Christmas week. The young people were to be indulged with a little dance; and although neither John nor Frederick knew much about dancing, they were pleased at the idea of joining with those who did, and already began to talk over the little young ladies of the neighbourhood, and to settle with whom they would, and with whom they would not dance.

They came home quite tired, and only in time to have their dress changed before dinner. Harriet and Elizabeth thought they had been absent a long while, and on their return into the drawing-room, were ready with their smiling countenances to receive these dear boys.

The next morning after breakfast, Mr. Mortimer employed a few hours in examining his boys in the improvements they had made during the last half-year; for he had wisely resolved, for the comfort of the whole family, that the entire day was not to be given up to play. During this time, Harriet and Elizabeth were occupied with their mamma; and after this as the day continued bright, though cold, it was determined to put into effect the proposed stroll of yesterday. And first to the farm-yard, where the poultry-maid supplied them with corn: and with this enticement, the fowls and ducks were called together and numbered, and the various beauties of both enumerated. This speckled hen had been such a good mother, and a good handful of grain was tossed to her;—then the beautiful little bantam had been nursed in a stocking, and was so tame that it would come and eat out of the hand;—then there was the fine old cock that crowed so loud he might be heard all over the parish, and a handful was thrown to him;—then there was the young one which the old one drove about so, that it could get nothing to eat;—Harriet made his necessities her care: but it was useless to throw him any: for the old cock would not allow him to come near the grain.

'Nasty greedy fellow,' said Elizabeth, 'I am sure there is enough for all, but the young cock cannot get a morsel.'

'I believe we must get rid of him,' observed Mrs. Mortimer; 'for it is miserable to see him driven about so.'

'He is to be killed next, Madam,' answered the poultry-maid, who now approached with two fowls hanging from her hands, from which drops of blood were falling.

Mrs. Mortimer moved away with the children: for she saw that Harriet turned pale at the sight of the blood.

'I cannot think how Jane can kill the fowls, mamma,' said Elizabeth; 'I am sure I could not, if we never had any at all.'

'I should be very sorry if you could, my dear little girl, for there is no necessity for your doing it; and without conquering your feelings of tenderness, you never could acquire the resolution to do it. In Jane's situation it was necessary for her to habituate herself to an employment which devolves to her as the rearer of the poultry: but I assure you it was a long time before she could first bring herself to deprive those creatures of life which she had been accustomed to look after and feed. And even now I believe when she can meet with the gardener or groom, she most generally employs them.'

'Are there no ducks, mamma?' said Frederick: 'we used to have such a number.'

'There is your old favourite drake just stopping under the gate,' replied Mrs. Mortimer: 'and we will follow him into the field, for it is rather cold standing still.'

They then went into the field, and after that came round to the green-house, where the gardener was very busily employed in gathering some beautiful grapes.

'How nice and warm it is here,' said several of the children, on entering the house. The gardener then approached to ask the young gentlemen how they did, and to tell them how much they were grown, and to say that he hoped they would like the grapes. John and Frederick answered all the old man's questions with kindness and civility; and as the young party were leaving the green-house, he asked them whether they should not want some flowers and evergreens against their little dance?

'Oh yes, if you please, gardener,' was the ready and quick answer:—'we may, mamma, may we not?' said Harriet, looking up at her mother before she gave her reply.

'The gardener may give you what he can spare,' replied Mrs. Mortimer. 'And gardener,' added she, looking back towards the green-house, 'desire your grandson to go into the copses, and bring home a little cart of holly, that we may have the kitchen well ornamented, when the tenantry come to their dinner.'

'He shall be sure to do it, ma'am,' replied the gardener. 'I look we shall have a merry Christmas, and I do like to see the room well dressed up.'

As Tom, the gardener's grandson, was a steady, well-behaved lad, Mrs. Mortimer allowed John and Frederick to accompany him to the copses, in search of the holly. Harriet and Elizabeth would, no doubt, very much have liked to belong to the party also, but they were easily convinced of the propriety of their not doing so, and were therefore satisfied to see their brothers drive off with Tom Harding, and return in two or three hours afterwards, walking by the side of the little vehicle, which then appeared a moving shrub of red-berried holly.

On Christmas-day the expected party met round the hospitable dinner-table of Mr. Mortimer, having all of them arrived on the preceding day at the grove, excepting the other branch of the Mortimer family, who attended their own parish church in the morning, and did not arrive till the hour of dinner.

The children of the village school, all in their new clothes, and with a sprig of holly in their bosoms and button holes, walked from the church to the Grove; and there partook, as they had been invited to do, of beef and pudding, and good home-brewed beer. The young Mortimers waited upon them at dinner, and before they left the Lodge, presented them each with a plumb cake; and Mrs. Mortimer gave them each an amusing little book to read to themselves and their parents, who had not like themselves possessed the advantages of learning to read.

The family dinner party went off as happily as that in the kitchen. The young Mortimers all sat together at the side table, and their papa, had not once occasion to call them out for being noisy, though they were merry and cheerful enough. It was certainly true, as Harriet had said, that her cousins would be noisy; on this day, however, being dispersed amongst the party at the large table, they were very orderly and well-behaved; and after dinner, when the young people had had taken as much fruit as was good for them, they retired into their play-room together: they sat round the blazing fire there provided for them, very comfortably and happily, and without one word of dissension till they were again called back for tea into the drawing room.

The next day was the day appointed for the dinner of the tenantry, and busy indeed were the young Mortimers, in dressing up the Hall, and making it look smart and lively. A very large party assembled here to enjoy the squire's hospitable table, at which he himself presided; and the day after this, the labouring cottagers and their wives met in the same room at one o'clock, round a table well covered with meat pies, legs of mutton, roast beef, potatoes, and plum pudding. They brought with them those of their children, who were too young to be in the school: and, on this occasion, all the new round frocks, and cotton gowns were exhibited. Little Frederick led his nurse up to the head of the table, and was very attentive to her; and whenever her plate was empty, he took care that it should not remain long so.

This party went off as happily as the last; and two days after was to take place the little dance, so anxiously looked forward to, not only by the Mortimers, but by all the young people in the neighbourhood. The Wexfords came very early in the morning, to assist their young friends in preparing the ball-room: and the gardener had taken good care to provide plenty of shrubs and flowers, for the necessary decoration. Mrs. Mortimer lent her assistance where it was required, and she was only fearful that the children would tire themselves before the pleasure of the evening commenced; for Mr. Mortimer had now pronounced the sheet of water in the park sufficiently frozen to bear any weight that might be ventured on it; and he had given several village lads permission to slide there, and prepare it for the use of his own boys. He now called upon both his own lads, and the young Wexfords, to join him, and for John he had provided a pair of skates. John met with a great many tumbles, to the amusement, not only of himself, but of his companions; but he had no serious bruises, and soon jumped up and laughed at his own awkwardness. Frederick longed to try the skates out. Mr. Mortimer thought him too little to venture upon them, so that he was obliged to be satisfied with sliding. And very prettily he did slide, and very much did Elizabeth wish to slide with him; for she was indeed a merry little girl, besides being always desirous of doing every thing which she saw her brother Frederick engaged in. But mamma thought it not a very fit amusement for little girls; so Elizabeth joined Harriet and the Miss Wexfords in a run round the park, all of them occasionally returning to the ice, to see how the skaters and sliders went on.

The hour of dinner was a very early one on this day, for the evening party was to be an early one. The young people, with their papas and mammas began to assemble at a very unfashionable hour, as early indeed as seven o'clock, and by eight they were all dancing away very merrily. Dancing was kept up with great spirit till towards eleven, when there was a summons to supper. Another hour was spent in taking refreshments, and during this time there was much merriment, and many jokes passing round, as well amongst the elder part of the assembly, as in that with which we are more particularly interested. Soon after twelve the party began to separate;—all had appeared to be very well satisfied with the pleasure they had been enjoying;—every one seemed in high good-humour and glee; and all the young visitors, as well as the four Mortimers, joined in acknowledging that the dance had gone off very well indeed; and in pronouncing that certainly 'Christmas was a very happy time.'

The End